Im Anfang war die Tat [Faust]

Prometheica created by
Polemos Editrice

Translated from Italian by A. Brandi
Logo N.

Layout FB
Polemos editrice
Oct. 2024

POLEMOS
editrice

https://polemos.info/

www.prometheica.it

PROMETHEICA

Review of studies on superhumanism, technology and European identity

Forging the New Era

Adinolfi ⏐ Anselmo ⏐ Boco ⏐ Scianca

VOLUME ONE

2024

POLEMOS
editrice

CONTENTS

«We're gonna transcend them»: Accelerationism Overcoming the Katechon

Adriano Scianca

«Hey, Doc, you better back up, we don't have enough road to get up to 88». «Roads? Where we're going, we don't need roads». This is the famous close from *Back to the Future*. The scene is well-known: Doc comes back from the future and asks Marty and his girlfriend to follow him «back to the future» to save their children. But the time machine, the modified DeLorean, only activates its mechanism at a speed of 88 miles per hour. There, in the back street by their house, there is no room to reach that speed. However, Doc surprises the kids by showing them that the car can fly. Acceleration is possible: *upwards*. Kinetic metaphors have often been used to describe a contemporary world out of control, even though they mostly refer to a train with no conductor: a society that constantly accelerates but is not really going anywhere except a precipice. Are we really sure this is the case, though?

The stagnant

That ride, perhaps, has already come to a stop. On closer inspection, in fact, we are living today in the age of the stagnant. Stagnant are the left and right wing, conservatives and progressives as well: despite its paraded dynamism, the ruling ideology and the system of power innervating it are about as stuck and static as one can get. An ideology dense with taboos, prohibitions, phobias, gripped by moral restraints and a monotheistic heritage that has never been overcome, timorous of ideological and political ghosts and that at this point is only able to conceive its own legitimacy in terms of negative thinking and police control.

The very same accelerating power of capitalism, the «highly revolutionary» function Marx attributed to bourgeoisie in history, appear to belong to a long-gone phase. Aside from histrionic tycoons such as Elon Musk capitalism today does not seem to be harbinger of a somewhat propulsive force, of a potential to take us towards an 'elsewhere'. On the opposite, the consumer of the third millennium is more and more sedentary: Netflix takes the cinemas among the domestic walls, Facebook allows social relationships without moving from one's room, Amazon delivers every type of goods to one's home, Deliveroo brings food and Pornhub puts sex at one's fingertips. Technology today does not gift us the beauty of velocity, but the praise of immobility. Donny Dorling, professor of Geography at Oxford, has recently sung the praises of the Great Slowdown that is supposed to take the place of modernity's Great Acceleration in progress at the moment. We are not aware of it, explains the British scholar, but from the cultural, ecological and demographic point of view we are already slowing down. Even in the field of technology Dorling is convinced we are about to come to a stop. As for what concerns the immediate future «they are most likely to be the enhancements of old technologies, such as batteries, and not the inventions of new ones, such as teleportation»[1]. Even the first law of Moore, according to which the complexity of a microcircuit doubles every 18 months and excited the imagination of techno-enthusiastic authors and the quick prophets of technological singularity, is apparently showing its structural limits.

«For my children», Dorling writes, «it is all far more convenient and works far more smoothly, but they were not among the first to be able to send an email or stand in a field and make a telephone call—I was. Selecting a track to listen to on Spotify or being able to choose a movie to watch on demand is not quite so mind-blowing as the technological changes in the 1970s and 1980s were for me—for them, it is just normal, because for them this is now commonplace. They have what billions of others have—a common technology. No longer are our children standing on the edge of acceleration looking forward into the utterly unknown»[2]. As it is evident, the diagnosis goes hand in hand with a precise ideological choice («slowing down is a very good thing»[3], «we have to stop seeing stagnation as an ill»[4]) and with a straightforwardly anti-futurist epic: «standing on the edge of acceleration looking forward into the utterly unknown» is an image Marinetti would have appreciated, not unlikely from that «defiance at the stars» cast from «promontory of the centuries».

The German sociologist Hartmut Rosa, from his end, despite providing a descriptively opposite interpretation

1   Danny Dorling, *Slowdown. The End of the Great Acceleration-and Why It's Good for the Planet, the Economy, and Our Lives*, Yale University Press 2020, p. 86.

2   Ibid., p. 88.

3   Ibid, p. 2.

4   Ibid., p. 8.

to Dorling's (however normatively identical – according to Rosa the acceleration is in progress but it allegedly is a catastrophe) admitted that «in late-modern society we find signs of strange processes, or perceptions, that suggest how, differently from the widespread phenomena of acceleration and flexibility – which create an apparent of a total contingency with endless options among which to choose an unlimited openness to the future – "real" change is no longer possible and how the system of modern society is closing and history is coming to an end that has a form of "hyper-accelerated standstill" or "polar inertia". Advocates of such a diagnosis of late modern "acceleration societies" are Paul Virilio, Jean Baudrillard, Fredric Jameson or Francis Fukuyama. They all claim there are no new visions and energies (first of all "utopic energies") and that is why the incredible speed of events and alteration is in reality simply a superficial phenomenon that hardly hides the structural and cultural inertia deeply rooted in the depths of our age»[5].

If Dorling and Rosa diverge in their analysis but converge in their core values, other authors are on the opposite side of the barricade. Stefano Vaj as well, for example, paints a sombre picture of deceleration but draws absolutely opposite conclusions that are ethical and have political and metapolitical consequences. As a matter of fact, Vaj too sees in our age a phase of stagnation: «Speed? In reality» writes the Milan-born author in a text from 2009, year of the centenary of the Manifesto of Futurism, «speed records have been basically stationary for decades. The absolute one, in space (which is still held by the Voyager, that has been travelling for more than thirty

---

5   Hartmut Rosa, *Alienation and Acceleration: Towards a Critical Theory of Late-modern Temporality*, NSU Press 2010, p. 38 (TN: adapted by the translator).

years). In the air, on the water, on wheels, on foot. Even more stationary, or decreasing, is the average speed of air, land and water transport. The European citizen who in the Eighties could cross the Atlantic on a Concorde is now approaching is retirement age [...]. "Flying cars" or the "helicopter in every garage" of the futurology of the Sixties are stuck on the yellowed pages of this type of literature, like the hovercrafts that were destined to replace ships on the world's oceans. If anything, we have cars that consume a little less, pollute a little less, are a little more aerodynamic».

As for technological transformations and *the 'magnificent and progressive fate of the human race'*, Vaj writes, «the first nuclear fusion plant was planned for the Eighties [...].. The "war on cancer" mostly generated a lot of statistics showing that thanks to advance diagnostics to average life expectancy of a patient has extended...because cancer patients used to discover their condition much later, and therefore did not enter the statistics. The first human landing on Mars had been confidently predicted for 1982 when Armstrong and Aldrin moved their first steps on the Moon, considering the technology of the time»[6]. According to Vaj, this scenario determines a veritable betrayal of the Futurist and Faustian heritage, if not of the entire anthropological parabola that started with the Neolithic revolution. Even science-fiction, despite possessing all the potential to be the vanguard of a new Futurist epic, generally does nothing but amplify ancestral fears and humanist-reactionary tendencies. «Science-fiction», wrote Daniel Dinello, «shows the transformation into the posthuman as the horrific harbinger of the long

---

6   Stefano Vaj, *I sentieri della tecnica*, Centro produzioni Moira, Milano 2021, 128-130 (TN: Translated into English for this publication).

twilight and decline of the human species. In its obsession with mad scientists, rampaging robots, killer clones, cutthroat cyborgs, human-hating androids, satanic supercomputers, carnivore virus and genetically-modified monsters, science-fiction expresses the technophobic fear to give away our human identity, our freedom, our emotions, our values and our lives to machines»[7]. Different messages have been mere slips such as *Blade Runner* or a few authors such as the Nolan brothers.

Zombie conservatism

However, the objective deceleration according to some is not enough. Every contrary temptation needs to be monitored and punished. It is not by chance if «official» thinkers of the establishment such as Jürgen Habermas[8], Francis Fukuyama[9], the liberal philosopher Michael John Sandel[10] (George W. Bush's bioethics expert), Leon Kass[11], the Vatican, all the conservative galaxy and a good part of left-wing intelligentsia[12] see in the possible posthuman transformation the utmost bugbear, feeling a

7   Daniel Dinello, *Technophobia! Science fiction visions of posthuman technology*, University of texas press, Austin, 2005, p. 2.

8   Jürgen Habermas, *The Future of Human Nature*, Polity, 2003.

9   Francis Fukuyama, *Our Posthuman Future: Consequences of the Biotechnology Revolution*, Picador, 2003.

10   Michael John Sandel, *The Case Against Perfection: Ethics in the Age of Genetic Engineering*, Cambridge: Harvard University Press, 2007.

11   Leon Kass, *Life, Liberty, and the Defense of Dignity: The Challenge for Bioethics*, Encounter Books, 2004.

12   A review of the various humanist and technophobic currents hostile to posthuman transformation can be found (TN: in Italian language) in Riccardo Campa, *Mutare o perire. La sfida del transumanesimo*, Sestante 2010 and in Maurizio Balistreri, *Superumani*, Espress, Torino 2020.

growing discomfort against certain possible technological developments. What is more incredible though is that many allegedly anti-conformists are following this trend. Despite the fact that the system seems definitely bogged down in its own contradictions, more and more of its opponents appear to be seduced by the inertial «solution» (going forward, certainly, but unhurriedly, possibly waiting for a future standstill and, why not, a desirable movement backwards). The inertial, decelerationist temptation innervates what we might call *zombie conservatism*, namely the desperate existential and political holding on to the larval remnants of an old world, refusing to take responsibility for moving beyond it. All of their bets are on an old order still standing but totally devoid of vitality: an actual living dead. Wagering everything on slowness or even on a standstill is obviously suicidal: not only there is no such a thing as a «natural» rhythm but, even fantasising impossible movements backwards, one could not know where to go back to, if not to the previous stop of a platform that has always the same terminus. Some examples of zombie conservatism:

On the discursive level: this is the approach of those who stand against what is politically correct, contrasting it with a «common sense» that has already been deconstructed, without grasping the radical nature of the challenges at hand, simply relying on the friction that «common sense» pitches against «subversive» ideologies (i.e. people persevering in using expressions today deemed offensive). *On the memorial level*: this is the opposition to *cancel culture* from those who believe they can avoid the battle for the past, relying on a de-politicized ecumenical and a-conflictual interpretation of history. *On the identity level*: this is the answer to the *critical race theory*, that brings back to life an identity which is taken for granted and simplified, thus escaping the total politicization of our history, in the perennial nostalgia of an age when such issues «were not even raised», «they did not constitute a problem».

On the anthropological level: this is the answer to the gender ideology, that solely relies on the resistance of «traditional» forms of relationships, relations and genders, against the transformations and the ideologies that aim to question them, with the objective of «freezing» them for the longest time possible («if our grandparents did so, why can't we?»).

On the economic level: this is the «solution» devised by those who want to prevent economic crises and environmental catastrophes, relying on the demobilizing myth of degrowth and to the voluntary (and global?) reduction of production and consumption.

On the ecologic level: This is the «politically active» posture of the Greta Thunberg generation's environmentalism of «small gestures», populated by young and frowning guards of turned off water taps, well represented in the film *L'heure de la sortie* by Sébastien Marnier. The inability to face the challenges of the present, trying on the opposite to slow them down, go around them, elude them, also leads to the naïve quest for the «oasis of authenticity»[13], namely places unstained by the decadence and modernity, where to actually, or more often, oneirically, find refuge: political-sovereignist oasis (Putin's Russia, Orban's Hungary), catholic-conservatist oasis (the Poland of bigotry), Islamo-revolutionary oasis (Ayatollahs' Iran), Islamo-primitivist oasis (Taleban Afghan-

13   This is, however, a false idea of authenticity, as Heidegger had already warned that *Eigentlichkeit* is the ability to decide one's own existential possibility in constantly open ways, which do not stand for the conservation of a final order (even though the later Heidegger, folded in his pastoral idyll, can have sometimes contributed to further the misunderstanding).

istan), late-communist oasis (Castro's Cuba), Sanfedista oasis («deep France», «deep America», etc.), spiritualistic-antimodernist oasis (Tibet, India or God knows which ignored tribe yet to be contaminated by modernity). All places and experiences that are idealised in an abstract, a-historical manner, maybe with the support of a returning Guénonian grandeur («the search for Agarthi»…) and end with eschatological delusions for which it suffices for a political leader to express an antiliberal opinion for him to get a historical-cosmic role: not a statesman anymore, but a force that «binds» the Antichrist…

Primum retardare

As a matter of fact, it has been the Catholic right-wing to have taken the decelerationist anxiety to the extreme, digging up from the Scriptures the mysterious figure of the *katechon*. As it is known, the *katechon* is a character appearing in St. Paul's *Second Epistle to the Thessalonians*, where it is reported that the end of times would have had to do with two disturbing and unclear characters, the man of anomia (*anomos*) and «the one (or 'that') who withholds»: the *katechon*. According to St. Paul, before the Parousia, or the second and last coming of Christ, utter evil would manifest, opposed by a figure whose task would be to «withhold» evil (the verb *katecho* means exactly «to withhold», «to prevent»). This power is however destined to succumb, leaving the path clear for apostasy, which will in turn be defeated by Christ. The *anomos* has traditionally been interpreted as the Antichrist, even though the word is not present in St. Paul's writings, while the exegetists have identified the *katechon* with the Church itself or the Roman Empire. The latter is also Carl Schmitt's opinion: «*ho katechon* is the *imperator* who time after time rules, while *to katechon* is the imperium. As long as the *imperium* exists, the world will not end»[14].

In more recent times the theme of the *katechon* has been connected with the resignation of the «traditionalist» Pope Benedict XVI and the coming of his successor, the «globalist» Francesco, respectively – and hurriedly – interpreted as the katechontic force and the incarnation of anomia. We know how Ratzinger has over the years pondered on such eschatological problems[15]. Conversely, Bergoglio appeared to many Catholic conservatists as the plastic representation of realised impiety, which the Scriptures say will present itself as a monkey of what is sacred. We are not interested in the least in this debate, if not to underline how the Ratzinger-Bergoglio dualism is central in the sovereignist imaginary and narrative and how much it has contributed to revamp (even in extra-religious terms) the katechontic theme, attuning a whole political and cultural discourse on the language of the «slowdown». It is sufficient to browse the internet to un-

---

14   Carl Schmitt, *Imperium*, Quodlibet, Macerata 2015, p. 70 (TN: translated into English for this publication). Developed starting from 1932, the concept of the katechon appears in Schmitt's writings only 10 years later, in 1942, in an article published in *Das Reich* and entitled (TN: in Italian) «Acceleratori involontari. Ovvero: la problematica dell'emisfero occidentale» (now in *Stato, grande spazio, nomos*, Adelphi, Milano 2015). However, the jurist would delve into this category especially in his post-war writings.

15   On this topic, cf. Giorgio Agamben, *The Mystery of Evil: Benedict XVI and the End of Days* Stanford University Press, 2017. In 1956, the then thirty-year-old Joseph Ratzinger had already published in the *Revue des Études augustiniennes* an articole on Ticonius, the Roman Donatist who had made a distinction between a black Church (*fusca*), made of evil peple, and a just Church (*decora*), made of those faithful to Christ, linking his thoughtcvs to the theme of the *katechon*. Decades later, in the general audience of 22 Aprl 2009, the German theologian – now Benedict XVI, again evoked the figure of Ticonius in relation to how we need to undestand «the mystery of the Church» today.

derstand the extent to which the sovereignist and conservatist answer to the challenges of globalism feeds on katechontic suggestions, may them be directly connected to the figure of the German Pope emeritus or not. Let us think of the use of the katechontic theme that an influential freelance journalist of the Catholic traditionalism such Maurizio Blondet[16] makes: a veritable metapolitical grammar takes form here and it tends to influence more and more sectors among those opposing globalist ideologies. *Primum retardare.*

However, it was Massimo Cacciari, in a dense essay[17] dedicated to the very emblematic figure quoted in the *Epistle to the Thessalonians* to underline how the *katechon* actively participates in the very principle it intends to withhold. As a matter of fact we have seen how the withholding force has no hope of winning on impiety, the outcome of the game has never been under discussion, history is not open to change. That is also why Cacciari refuses the identification of the *katechon* with the Imperium, the latter being a figure impossible to link to any messianic time, any eschatological historical framework. According to Cacciari, this is not the age for a possible imperial *katechon*, this is the age of Epimetheus, literally the age that «cannot predict», «cannot plan», just like the politician who deludes himself into thinking to «withhold» the economic-technical impiety[18]. All one has left to do is to

---

16   We are referring to his famous and controversial essay on *Gli "Adelphi" della dissoluzione* (Ares, Milano 1994), where the welding between the «right-wing» philosophical traditionalis and the «left-wing» cultural dyonisism came to embody the anti-katechontic character of an anti-christic acceleration. Blondet has then written on the topic of the *katechon* in dozens of other essays and articles.

17   Cf. *The Withholding Power. An Essay on Political Theology*, Bloomsbury Academic, 2018.

18   Cf. ibid.

wager on the other brother, on Prometheus. All one has left to do is to accelerate.

Accelerate!

As is known, Accelerationism is the name of a philosophical current which originated in the Nineties around the mythical CCRU, the Cybernetic Culture Research Unit of the English Warwick University, animated by the visionary and controversial Nick Land, and that later gave birth to several currents, some «right-wing» ones («the black enlightenment» originated by Land himself), some «left-wing» ones (such as the revisited Marxism by Mark Fisher). The fundamental intuition is that of abandoning any illusions of leaving the technological and capitalist system, any pastoral nostalgia, in order to push – on the opposite – the process to its extreme consequences, convinced that alienation, once set at its maximum speed, can generate a new universe of meaning of a definitely post-humanist nature. «The point of an analysis of capitalism, or of nihilism», Land writes, «is to do more of it. The process is not to be critiqued. The process is the critique, feeding back into itself, as it escalates. The only way forward is through, which means further in»[19].

Beyond Land and associates' tenets, for that matter quite involute, for us the Promethean accelerationism means to intensify the research on biotechnology, cognitive sciences, robotics, nanotechnology, cloning, assisted procreation, mind uploading, genomic editing, artificial procreation and technological singularity, creatively and actively taking responsibility for the challenges of humanism and its consequences; to intensively use such

---

19   Nick Land, «A Quick-and-Dirty Introduction to Accelerationism», in *A Nick Land reader. Selected writings*, s.e, s.d, p. 35.

technologies to implement demographic, ecological, identitary, power and sovereignty policies; to acknowledge the irreversible crisis of political institutions and the narratives based on the triad «God, Country, Family», to be brave enough to write new tablets inspired by our ancestral origins, albeit in a radically new and «imperial» forms according to the previously mentioned meaning. There is nothing to be conserved, everything has to be reinvented anew. No going back: there is only forward. The archaeology of the concept of Accelerationism is however enlightening. The idea came to the mind of the young English philosophers when they read a passage Gilles Deleuze and Felix Guattari's *Anti-Oedipus*: «But which is the revolutionary path? Is there one? —To withdraw from the world market, as Samir Amin advises Third World countries to do, in a curious revival of the fascist "economic solution"? Or might it be to go in the opposite direction? To go still further, that is, in the movement of the market, of decoding and deterritorialization? For perhaps the flows are not yet deterritorialized enough, not decoded enough, from the viewpoint of a theory and a practice of a highly schizophrenic character. Not to withdraw from the process, but to go further, to "accelerate the process," as Nietzsche put it»[20] .

The fundamental idea is that of a capitalism able to unleash powerful flows of desire, destroyers of bonds and hierarchies but that always returns to «reterritorialize», namely to reproduce new orders and power relationships. Hence the idea to intensify those flows internal to capitalism to eventually turn them against capitalism itself. Where did exactly Nietzsche invite to «accelerate the process» of modernity, though? We need to refer to

---

20   Gilles Deleuze, Felix Guattari, *Anti-Oedipus*, University of Minnesota press, 1983, pp. 239-240.

the fragment (105) 9 [153], entitled *The Strong of the Future*, dating back to autumn 1887. Quite interestingly, here the German philosopher does not write about capitalism nor modernity, but investigates the conditions for «the breeding of a *stronger race*». Well, for Nietzsche the point is not to fight homogenising, but taking it to its more radical consequences, so to generate a surplus of energy unabsorbed by the human herd and then destined to justify a higher humanity: «the *homogenizing* of European man is the great process that cannot be obstructed: one should even hasten it. The necessity *to create a gulf, distance, order of rank*, is given eo ipso-- not the necessity to retard this process[21]». The verb that Sossio Giametta translates as «affrettare»[22] is *beschleunigen* in the original, translated by Klossowski in his influential *Nietzsche et le cercle vicieux* from 1969 as *accélérer*[23]. The genealogy is now clear: from Nietzche to Klossowski, from Klossowski to Deleuze and Guattari, from Deleuze and Guattari to accelerationists, even though, in the various passages the meaning, direction and contents of acceleration seem different.

The concept can also bring to mind the well-known auspice by Julius Evola, according to which one should not fight the collapse of the bourgeois society, but needs to act «accelerating the rhythm of "progress", waiting for the end, or, if this is not enough, going too far as to pro-

---

21   Walter Kaufmann, *The Will to Power*, Random House, NY, 1967 (The author quotes the Italian translation – including the words in italics - by Giametta, in: Friedrich Nietzsche, *Opere*, vol. VIII, tomo II, *Frammenti postumi 1887-1888*, Adelphi, Milano 1971, pp. 78-79).

22   (TN: "hasten" in Kaufmann's translation).

23   *Obsolete Capitalism - Deleuze and the Algorithm of the Revolution*, https://onscenes.weebly.com/philosophy/deleuze-and-the-algorithm-of-the-revolution.

voke it, so that the ground is clear for the instant rise of the new tree»[24] (resolution clashing with his later, more markedly katechontic suggestions, such as political openness to the Church «if only was still the one of the Syllabus of Errors» or the military and monarchic world)[25]. However, the concept possesses, in Evola and especially among his readers, a fundamental ambiguity, as it is possible to read in it a purely regressive desire, namely the idea to come to the «end of a cycle» and restore a metaphysical and existential meaning, maybe in pastoral-idyllic terms, with the return of a new «golden age», a world where God «is dead no more». Hence, it is the Guénonian idea of modernity as a sort of techno-militant hangover one is eventually destined to get over and restore «true values». Accelerationism, on the opposite, does not see the acceleration as a means to come as quickly as possible to a new standstill, an oasis of meaning, but has in the very same acceleration its own meaning. However, in Evola, and especially in the Evola who read Jünger's *Worker*[26] there is also the possibility to go beyond modernity, by accelerating its own contradictions and mastering its apparently more alienating characteristics, such as «total mobilisation».

Apropos Jünger, it is useful to remember that after all it was him who provided the best definition of accelerationism, quite interestingly not in his more Promethe-

---

24   Julius Evola, *Pagan Imperialism*, Gornahoor Press, 2017, p. 84.

25   Sandro Consolato dedicated an important essay to the compresence of these two possibilities (plus a third one, which is the one of individual, ascetic rebelliousness): «Le "tre soluzioni" di Julius Evola», in *Le tre soluzioni di Julius Evola e altri studi evoliani*, Arya, Genova 2020.

26   Julius Evola, *The 'Worker' in the Thought of Ernst Jünger*, https://evolaasheis.wordpress.com/2016/04/14/the-worker-in-the-thought-of-ernst-junger-extract/.

an writings, but in his senile and so to say «Apollonian» period: «with the twenty-first century» said the German philosopher in the Nineties, «we will enter in a new age of Titans, characterised by the release of a gigantic amount of energy. I am thinking first and foremost about atomic energy, but also about how much energy will be necessary to meet the needs of a constantly growing world population. The plant will experience an acceleration *mankind will have to cope with by transforming itself.* The old will have to give way to the new. This is why the Worker will still be the adequate human form for the new reality»[27].

Trascending modernity.

One can certainly ask what accelerating accelerationism really means. The delivery boy obliged to deliver goods at a client's home within 10 minutes from the order or the occasional worker who is forced by a shipping multinational to urinate in his trousers in order not to slow down the chain of production represent a pathological, merely quantitative «acceleration» of the current system, which can easily coexist with an actual political and technological standstill. The same increase in the speed of cars, airplanes, processors, is more of a collateral consequence than the essence of accelerationism: despite creating changes that are also quantitative in nature, acceleration is an exquisitely qualitative phenomenon. The essence of accelerationism concerns the *pro* of *promethéuomai* («to predict», «to provide»), namely the «before», the «forward» that gives a perspective to the

---

27   Antonio Gnoli and Franco Volpi, *I prossimi Titani. Conversazioni con Ernst Jünger*, Adelphi, Milano 1997, p. 105. Italics by the author. (TN: translated from Italian for this publication).

methis, the vibrating and audacious cunning, the resolutive and creative intellect. It is that *pro* that needs to be accelerated: forward! Looking forward, moving forward: accelerationism is especially the radical will to go beyond the current state of things and its essential aspects from the political, spiritual, economic, anthropologic, ontological points of view. As is evident, this has nothing to do with the simple speeding up of the internal dynamics to such social and existential structures.

Perhaps, once reached this point, the concept of acceleration itself, so one-dimensional, does not do justice to this contradiction we need to solve, to this conflict we need to get through.

Acceleration only shows a way, an already mapped path. Perhaps one needs not only to accelerate illuministic modernity, but to transcend it (from the Latin *transcendere* «go beyond, ride on», made of *trans*, «through», and *scandere* «come up, climb, elevate»). Modernity has to be transcended, therefore passed through, including its fakest and most alienating aspects, but with a going through that is also a going beyond, leaving the fetishes of Western Humanism in the rearview mirror.

One does not have to «resist» globalism, there is nothing to be «withheld» or «delayed», one needs to have the courage to think what comes next and push down on the accelerator until all the passengers unfasten their seatbelts and start preying, until the «progressives» beg to get off it, and then even further, where the roads are unmapped, until modernity and capitalism have transcended in something else which is its opposite, something higher[28].

---

28   This is also why this article must not be read (even though this is inevitably going to happen…) as a «nihilistic», «satanic» even!, invitation to dissolution – resolution that would be totally consistent

In *Transcendence*, a film from 2014 directed by Wally Pfister and produced by the visionary Christopher Nolan, the brilliant theorist of artificial intelligence and technological singularity Will Caster, played by Johnny Depp, completes a mind-uploading before dying, therefore becoming himself an artificial intelligence beyond his physical body. He appears to be the classic «mad scientist» of luddite science-fiction, even though the ending unveils a much more articulated, futuristic and lucid plan that anyone around him, friends or foes, had suspected. Surrounded and being shot at – and this is truly interesting – by anti-technological terrorists who had joined forces with government forces, accompanied by his girlfriend Evelyn, who warns him («We can't fight them»), Will, before connecting with the entire ecosystem, going beyond the dichotomy between what is natural and artificial, answers: «We're not gonna fight them. We're gonna transcend them».

---

with the ruling dialectics and would leave the existential forms of the current system «un-transcended». After all, the moralist and the immoralist both share the same moral framework...

PROMETHEUS:
"ACTIVE SIN" AS THE FOUNDATION
OF THE EUROPEAN SPIRIT

Carlomanno Adinolfi

*With the glory of passivity I now contrast the glory of activity
which illuminates the Prometheus of Aeschylus.*
F. Nietzsche, The Birth Of Tragedy.

*In fact, he has already tacitly implied that every act in the ma-
terial domain is limiting and that the highest spiritual sphere
is accessible only in ways different from those of action. In
this premise the influence of a vision of life is clearly recogni-
sable which, in its essence, remains strange to the spirit of the
Aryan race*
J. Evola, The Aryan Doctrine of Combat and Victory

Prometheus through the centuries

The figure of Prometheus has often been at the
center of a debate between scholars, poets and philosophers. Was it - or better yet, is, since Myth is eternal and ever present -a positive or negative figure?
Should we emphasize his push to lift Man from the
mud through the gift of celestial Fire? Or should he be

condemned instead since the theft from Olympus ultimately linked him to the immortal archetype of *hybris*,the most heinous wrong according to the Hellenes. Needless to say the answer will vary depending on the age, but even more so on the context in which it is found.

One of the most "modern" interpretations of the Prometheus' myth is certainly the one offered by Boccaccio in his *Genealogia Deorum Gentilium*, where the titan is presented as the symbolic knowledge liberating man from his primitive and brutal condition. In this context even the torture that Prometheus has to endure is no more indicative of a punishment but rather the very nature of the wise man, ever tormented by the thirst for quest and truth. Boccaccio proved also ahead of time as he introduced one of the main themes of a certain "hermetic" Renaissance which would follow up on one of Neoplatonism's most metaphysical and theurgical concepts, namely man's innate capability to attain divine knowledge. Not surprisingly Boccaccio's interpretation of the Promethean myth was resumed in *Quaestiones Quinque de Mente* by Marsilio Ficino, who translated the Promethean condition into that of the sage who, once he'd lit the spark of knowledge, finds himself more miserable than the nescient as he's now fully aware of his own natural limitations, limitations that by now he cannot but try and overcome. Giordano Bruno introduces a new view of Prometheus as a rebellious figure opposing religious and moral dogmas[1], although the philosopher from Nola considers the titan guilty of distributing the highest of gifts in a reckless way, when instead it should have been granted only to those deserving of it[2].

---

1   *Cabala del Cavallo Pegaseo.*

2   *In his Sigillus Sigillorum Giordano Bruno affirms: "Remember that Prometheus did not please the gods, for he spread out the gods' treasures,*

Amongst the most negative readings of Promethus, the one given during the Age of Enlightenment by Rousseau, who in his *Discours sur les sciences et les arts* turns the titan into the corrupter of man's natural state of happiness, the 'good savage' living harmoniously in a pre-civilised state discovers the flame of technology heralding misfortune and misery. This is also where we first encounter Prometheus at the very center of the debate on the utility of technology and progress and within which limits it should or shouldn't abide into, a debate which lasted for the whole of the Age of Enlightenment. With the arrival of Romanticism Prometheus enjoyed new found fortune, becoming the very symbol and key figure of the heroic revolt against two distinct forms of oppression, Enlightenment's rationalism on the one hand and religious, both catholic and protestant, sanctimonious fideism on the other. Goethe makes him the protagonist of his short poem *Prometheus*, which the German poet intended as a part of an homonymous drama, the original plan never materialized and all that remains of it are two acts. In it the titan becomes the demiurge and architect of the human greatness showing mankind that they are not the ones in need of Gods, but on the contrary it's the Gods whom are dependent upon the honours that the mortals offer them. The rebellious theme of the Promethean myth explodes during the English Romanticism with Lord Byron[3] and especially Percy Bysshe Shelley, who, in his lyrical drama *Prometheus Unbound*, inspired

by appearing to and awakening the sleeping human race, and by promiscuously making this most excellent thing common to both the noble and ignoble among them". In this vision we can perhaps recognise the influence that alchemical and mysteric doctrines had on Giordano Bruno in that they dictate the non disclosure of secrets unless one is either an initiate or someone deemed worthy.

3   *Prometheus*, poem composed in 1816.

by Aeschylus's, celebrates the titan's victory, the symbol of Humanity revolting against tyranny, dogma and all the shackles imposed by religious, political and moral authorities. The symbol of all that is Zeus the tyrant, bound to be overthrown to the make space to the new cosmic ruler, as foretold in a prophecy which only Prometheus knows: the Demogorgon[4]. A completely opposite vision is offered by the English poet's wife, Mary Wollstonecraft Godwin, better known as Mary Shelley[5], who made Prometheus the archetype of the failed attempt to make use of technology to go beyond the human limits. Her most popular novel, *Frankenstein*, is also known as *The Modern Prometheus* and is a condemnation aimed at the scientist who tries to be God breathing new life into dead matter. Carducci completely overturns this notion in his *The Two Titans*, making Prometheus the emblem of modernity, technology, vitalism and man's pioneering spirit able to vanquish religious dogmas, moral conservatisms and bigotries. Here the Italian poet returns to the themes found in his *A Hymn to Satan*, in which the demon becomes the symbol of everything condemned by Christian morality, from inebriation and sex to technology (that was the time when Pope Gregory XVI was railing out against the "infernal machine" namely the train). We begin to see here

---

4   The Demogorgon is a mythical figure whose first appearance as a primigenial and sovereign deity. According to Shelley he represents the Eternity into which everything is reconnected after the reign of Zeus, who defeating Chronos started the flow of time. But it is also the unspoken Speech, the untold Word, a primigenial power capable to regulate of governing Destiny itself. It's not unlikely then that the entirety of Shelley's work is rife with a highly metaphysical meaning. For more details on the figure of Demogorgon, cf *Il mito di Demogorgone*, Marco Barsacchi, Marsilio, 2014.

5   Daughter of Mary Wollstonecraft, considered by many the first feminist, author of *A Vindication of the Rights of Woman*, and of the anarcho - communist philosopher William Godwin.

a blurring distinction between the figure of Prometheus bringer of Fire and Lucifer bringer of Light, already present in Milton's *Paradise Lost* and later to be found in Mario Rapisardi's *Lucifer*. With Prometheus carrying the torch of man's knowledge and will, we start to see Prometheus engaged in a battle against the Church and by assimilation even God, opening the doors to luciferian interpretations which during the 20th century would bring forth a number of more or less satanical readings.

Nietzsche and the Promethean "active sin"

And again we are faced with the same initial question. Where does Prometheus's virtue end and where does his guilt begin? When the Promethean myth opens the way to paths leading astray instead of Olympus, is it then still desirable to make it one's own? One of the readings which help us better find our way out of this ostensible *cul de sac* is offered by the philosopher who more than anyone else succeeded in overcoming the moral dichotomy between good and evil. In his *The Birth of Tragedy* Nietzche makes the Promethean myth one of the pillars on which the whole European Weltanshauung is build upon. Perhaps in Prometheus stealing the celestial fire and forging man in his own image the German philosopher catches a glimpse of the prodromes of Superman, who is rule to himself and capable to create a world abiding by new tables of the law which he himself carved, but above all sees *"original possession of the entire Aryan family of races, and documentary evidence of their capacity for the profoundly tragic"*[6]. The action of Prometheus who takes control of the celestial power to give it to feral men blessing them with the will to go further, is an unnatural stretch creat-

---

6   F. Nietzsche, *The Birth of Tragedy*

ing a chasm between human and divine, but it's exactly this tragic stretch which constitutes the very essence of the European man, the source of the tension pushing him *higher and even further*[7] but most of all *"the power of these two worlds of suffering constraining to reconciliation, to metaphysical oneness"*[8] be the seed of a new civilisation, of a new path with the Gods: *"man, elevating himself to the rank of the Titans, acquires his culture by his own efforts, and compels the gods to unite with him, because in his self-sufficient wisdom he has their existence and their limits in his hand"*[9]. But it's also in the Promethean "punishment" that Nietzsche makes out the tragic essence of the European Man. The tragic end of Prometheus, is indeed anything but a punishment for a misdeed: it's the trial to which he's been subjected by the celestial Gods, the whole range of sufferings and hardships that needs to be endured to reach the supernal Olympian heights. *"The Titanic artist found in himself the daring belief that he could create men and at least destroy Olympian deities: namely, by his superior wisdom, for which, to be sure, he had to atone by eternal suffering. [...] The best and highest that men can acquire they obtain by a crime, and must now in their turn take upon themselves its consequences, namely the whole flood of sufferings and sorrows with which the offended celestials must visit the nobly aspiring race of man"*[10]. In this Nietzsche sees a "grade of kinship" with the original sin myth from the old testament, but there is a crucial dif-

---

7   D'Annunzio's motto addressed to the First group of aerial squadron. It is featured in the "plea" to the pilots written by the Poet on May 24th 1917 to urge them to accomplish even greater and harder endeavours.

8   Ibid.

9   Ibid.

10   Ibid.

ference. According to the Jewish myth, Abraham's defiance to God is the source of all evil, he is condemned with no appeal, it is sin *tout court*. Instead the idea of the divine sufferings burdening the mortal man on his way to Olympus is *"a bitter reflection, which, by the dignity it confers on crime, contrasts strangely with the Semitic myth of the fall of man, in which curiosity, beguilement, seducibility, wantonness,—in short, a whole series of pre-eminently feminine passions,—were regarded as the origin of evil"*[11]. The Prometheus concept is a new one, an *"Aryan representation"* which *"is the sublime view of active sin"*[12]. Active sin, the challenge to Heaven as the necessary driving force for European Civilisation, born after a new synthesis, a new resolution, a new Pax Deorum, at last this is an idea stirring things up when debating the titan. No longer do we see positive and negative, good or evil, moral or immoral: what really exists is the necessity to act and to face all the pains that stem from it and only those who can meet the challenges will be able to reach a new Nexus of Civilisation.

This idea will be resumed years later by Julius Evola. The Roman metaphysiacian reclaims the same nitzschean theories about sin, highlighting how, according to the Judeo-Christian tradition, the challenge aimed at God in the Garden of Eden is deemed to be the root of all evil, likewise the attempt to elevate oneself to the divine heights would be condemned as the gravest of sins. Instead, according to the Aryan conception, the only thing dividing the titan from the hero is to be found in their respective achievements: the first failed while the second made it to Olympus. Moreover: the titan is defined "the

---

11   Ibid.

12   Ibid.

prime matter out of which the hero is made"[13], suggesting that the very will to defy the Heavens, to confront the Gods, the thirst for heights and overcoming one's own limits are but necessary elements to whoever is willing to take the heroic path. In the absence of these factors, there would be no hero. It's up to the person undertaking this path not to be consumed by the unquenchable thirst for heights and not to perish overcome by the chains - this is the meaning behind Prometheus bound and tormented by an eagle lacerating his innards forever[14] - and instead reconcile with a higher celestial law capable of surpassing through a supreme synthesis the dichotomy human / divine and reach, like Hercules did, Olympus as Gods' honoured guest. Just like Hercules appearing in the Greek myth as the the one who sets Prometheus free reuniting him with the wronged Father of the Gods.

Hercules as fulfilment of Prometheus

Hercules himself is an often overlooked element, but especially in the myth of Prometheus he takes center stage. While especially during the European Romanticism the figure of Prometheus became the only protagonist of the myth thanks to his rebellious and vitalistic traits who proved highly fascinating for IX century's poets and intellectuals, it is however important to look at the original myth in order to pinpoint its most profound meaning and how crucially important it is for European civilisation.

In its highest expression, that of the Aeschylean tragedy, there is an unbreakable duality between the figures of Prometheus and Heracles. The absence of one ren-

13   J. Evola, *The Mystery of the Grail.*

14   J. Evola, *The Hermetic Tradition.*

ders the existence of the other completely useless. Evola, consistent with Nietzsche, grasps its significance. *"In the Hellenic-Achaean tradition, for instance, Heracles is described as a heroic prototype precisely in these terms. Heracles earns Olympian immortality after allying himself to Zeus, who is the Olympian principle, against the "giants"; according to one of the myths of this cycle, it is through Heracles that the "titanic" element (symbolized by Prometheus) is freed and reconciled with the Olympian element"*[15].

The Olympian hero is but the one with the capacity to free the titanic element, which is an essential step when embarking on the heroic journey. More than that: the true endeavour accomplished by Heracles winning over Olympus is the very "conciliation" Nietzsche had hoped for as necessary requirement for the birth of an European civilisation. *"The Titan represents one who does not accept the human condition and who wants to steal the divine fire. [...] The titanic type -or, in another respect, the warrior type- is, after all, the prime matter of which heroes are made. But in order to implement a positive solution to the dilemma, that is, to attain an Olympian transformation as the reintegration of the primordial state, it is necessary to fulfill a double condition. First of all, it is necessary to show the proof and the confirmation of the virile qualification; thus in the epic and knightly symbolism we find a series of adventures, feats, and fights. This qualification should not become a limitation, a hubris, a closure of the "I", and it should not paralyze the capability of opening oneself up to a transcendent force, in function of which alone can the fire really become light and free itself. Second, such liberation should not signify a cessation of the inner tension; thus a further test consists in adequately reaffirming the virile quality on the supersensible plane. The consequence of this is the Olympian transformation or the achievement of that dignity*

---

15   J. Evola, *The Mystery of the Grail.*

which in initiatory traditions has always been designated as regal"[16].

Nietzsche and Evola again find common ground when they both identify that "inner tension" with the tension of heights, the rejecting of one's own human condition, the will to be endowed with the divine power capable of shaping and be the guiding principle of new laws yet to be written, as essential condition to understand the European spirit. A condition in the absence of which the European civilisation as we have known it wouldn't have existed. Evola goes even further than the German philosopher offering a metaphysical explanation for that "conciliation" which is for both the other necessary condition. According to the Roman philosopher it's exactly that opening which allows for the turning of fire into light. In this symbolic allegory we are finding echoes of Indoaryan mythologies which can help us delve deeper into the Promethean (and herculean) mystery.

The aspects of Fire in the Indoaryan Myth

Fire, the element that Prometheus stole from the heavens, used to have a central role in Indoaryan religions. It was Hestia's hearth, whereas in the Vedas It was the sacrificial fire of Agni, who also constituted the connection between Men and Gods through sacrifice and heroic ascent[17]. It was the imperishable Fire granting the Pax Deorum, it was Vesta's in Rome and Zoroaster's in Avestic and modern Iran. But the Indoaryan traditions don't fail

---

16   Ibid.

17   "The path he [Agni]treads is black and white and red", Rgveda X, 20, 9. Perhaps in this instance, instead of the chromatic "threefold funcionality" suggested by Dumezil, we find the archetypal origin of what was to become the alchemical path nigredo-albedo-rubedo.

to acknowledge the most dangerous fire, devouring and consuming even infernal at times. However even in these contexts, the cult would greatly differ from the Semitic or Oriental conceptions of deities such as Moloch for instance, according to which the god resembled more an evil, or at least dark, demon.

Jean Haudry's *Loki*[18] presents the deceitful Norse god as a distant relative of Prometheus, a god whose field is the "qualifying word's fire', a fire which is inherently Indoeuropean, unscrupulous and equipped with an ardent eloquence. A perilous and ambiguous fire, which nevertheless gives shape, will and word, just like the Promethean fire.

Furthermore in Ragnarok Loki, who was chained to a rock and condemned to a corrosive torture just like Prometheus, will be the protagonist of the last duel, during which he will be facing the god Heimdall. The two Gods will annihilate each other, each one vanishing into the other. Many consider Heimdall a relative of Agni because of his function as a "means " between humans and Gods, since he's the one connecting the worlds through the iridescent bridge Bifrost. If that were the case we would see in Ragnarok, the timeless moment in which the opposites merge to give life to a new cycle, a devouring fire that in order to create a new world must assimilate itself into a celestial sacrificial fire. But Heimdall was also the "white god", since he's the lord of Bifrost, the rainbow refracting the solar radiance into the colours of the iris, which makes him a god of light. This feature in the clash-synthesis between Loki and Heimdall at the end of times echoes the words of Evola: *the capability of opening oneself up to a transcendent force, in function of which alone can the fire really become light and free itself.* Perhaps the most telling crux

---

18   *J. Haudry, Loki, ed. Polemos 2021.*

is to be found in the Roman myth and civilisation (myth itself).

Everyone is aware of Vesta's fire, which was meant to burn perpetually inside the round temple whose remains are still visible in the Forum, a little south of Caesar's Altar, not far from the Dioscuri's Temple. But few remember the fact that there was another everlasting fire in Rome: it was the one consecrated to the god Vulcan, which was burning in the Volcanal placed right next to the *Umbilicus Urbis*, the meeting point of the guidelines followed by Romolus when he traced the sacred borders of Rome. A cornerstone in all respects, where it appears the very first meetings of the Senate would take place during the royal age, before the Curia was built just meters away. That was the location of the *mundus* which Romolus devoted to the deities of the netherworld. And perhaps that was also where Romolus himself was buried. The spoils of war were offered to Vulcan, thrown in the fire so that they could be devoured in order to avoid any further use against Rome. But why an inherently devouring and destructive fire was given such a central role in Rome? A subterranean god by nature, thus inferior? And why was the very centre of Rome consecrated to deities of the netherworld? Actually there's nothing more normal than this. According to the Romans, and the Etruscans before them, the founding of a city equals a cosmogonic act. A city was but a Cosmos on a small scale. Rome, the city par excellance, certainly couldn't do any different. And a Cosmos is made up of the earth of the human events, the heavenly dome of the supernal Gods and the underworld dome of the inferior Gods. In the absence of even one of these elements, there would be no Cosmos but only Chaos. Obviously there is a clear and absolutely unchangeable hierarchy. That which lays below must submit to what is above. That which is inferior must then be integrated into an Order which abide by the Heavens. It's the same "conciliation" discussed at length by Nietzsche as well as Evola, the fulcrum which the Pax Deorum was founded upon, made manifest and guaranteed by Vesta's Fire. A very peculiar reading of the Italic myth of Vulcan and Prometheus is offered by Guido Di Nardo in his *Il preistorico culto infero del Vulcano laziale sul Campidoglio di Roma*[19]. In this perhaps more visionary than historically accurate pamphlet,which among other things culminates in a homage to the Demogorgon mentioned by Boccaccio as well as Shelley, the author imagines a primordial mankind and its prehistoric cults consecrated to an inferior deity of devouring fire, a Moloch from Lazio to whom human sacrifices were made, before the cult of Jupiter established itself to bring back that ordering conciliation in Olympian terms. One of the most interesting passages deals with the cosmogonic explanation of the cult envisioned by Di Nardo. He does indeed illustrate with absolute scientific rigor the formation of our planet: an emission of incandescent gas and cosmic fire detached from the Sun, which upon entry in the star's gravitational field concentrate while rotating around an axis, then cool down, while still retaining an inner core made of incandescent fire. Di Nardo sees in this the prefiguration of Prometheus and Vulcan's myth: the Celestial Fire's theft, which is the detachment of a part of the solar fire, to give life on earth. But it is indeed inside this stolen fire, this inferior fire, that we can find all that's necessary to have a knowledge of the divine Fire. The Promethean fire "bound" to the rock needs to be "liberated" in order to return to its original abode. That's why we see the

---

19   G. Di Nardo, *Il preistorico culto infero del Vulcano laziale sul Campidoglio di Roma*, Tip. G. Zampetti, 1942

emergence of the early cults dedicated to Cabeiri, Vulcan's helpers, masters of the secret art of metallurgy who served as foundations for all the cults of mystery and alchemy, which indeed call for the reunification with the solar principle through by means of secret and "subterranean" doctrines of fire mastery[20]. A vision that embraces the myth seeing Vulcan / Hephaestus forging not only Jupiter / Zeus' thunderbolts, but also the weapons of the hero who's been granted divine immortality. Hephaestus is the one forging Achille's divine weapons, Vulcan is the one forging Enea's divine weapons. If the inferior fire stolen from the Heavens were lacking, there would be no metallurgic craft and technology, without these it would be impossible to forge the weapons for the Hero, without Heroes civilisation couldn't exist. At least not the European one.

The moral refusal of technology as an anti-European archetype

This principle must matter especially today, in an time where technology has reached the point of permeating every aspect of our life, in the so called digital era where everyone of us is surrounded by high tech devices and where we witness a succession of revolutionary scientific discoveries day after day. To refuse technology, as it's unfortunately common nowadays, because it opens the doors to dystopian and dehumanizing sceneries is however a conception which is more modern than modernity itself, as it has no epigones in none of the thinkers or historical protagonists who can be considered fundamental to our ancient civilisation, but is instead just the flip side

---

20   See Vitriol, Latin acrostic meaning "Visit the interior of the earth and [by] purifying [yourself] you will find the hidden stone".

of the coin of modernistic thought. English luddites or zealots following the papal seals against "infernal machines" had both in themselves an anti-European seed, something that is missing in the likes of Carducci, who would exalt technology and life, Beethoven, who would glorify modern Europe (or what was considered modern back then), Goethe, who would celebrate knowledge or Marinetti, who would praise speed and technology as Promethean challenge to the stars. The revolt against the modern world that many pseudo-traditionalists are calling for while quoting Evola was never meant to be against progress, technology or science. If anything it's a revolt against progressivism and scientism and therefore against a certain mental and "spiritual" approach to technology, but never ever a conservatism designed to idealise a more bucolic past as well as a technological regress which was never part of the European spirit. The inviolable "sacredness of the human body" is a inherent drift of rural sects following the old testament and refusing cures while awaiting God's miracle, very much reminescent of the saying "If man were meant to fly, he would have been born with wings". The Indoeuropean man has always been bearer of innovation by means of technology. It is he who erected megalithic temples making use of technologies that we can't still figure out. It is he who invented war chariots and elevated metallurgy and the art of weapons to the highest levels, he was the first to "better" the inviolable human body adopting weapons and armours in the beginning and technical suits later on, he was the builder of the great classical temples, who invented arch structures, monumental edifices, cathedrals, who conceived perspective, who generated the most remarkable artistic currents in history, who designed the most complex machineries from Leonardo until the 20th century and much more. To think of a Greek or a Roman refusing technological progress because of some moral issues is like thinking of a beast refusing to hunt its preys not to hurt them: it is simply something unnatural and impossible. A Roman or a Hellene would have never refused genetic researches on the ground that they are abhorrent, instead they would have used them to improve future generations and cure illnesses, while obviously questioning the ensuing dangers and implications, the Hellene philosophising upon it whereas the Roman would enact iron laws in order to retain the Right, all of which while trying to master its technology. They would have never refused practices of assisted reproduction or fertility treatments feeling triggered by some obscure religious taboo, they would have certainly abhorred the idea of surrogacy markets and rainbow families, but never would they turn down the possibility of helping procreation. A Caesar or an Alexander would have never refused to advance digitalisation in all possible fields dreading a dystopia where connected subhumans are directed by whoever is in charge of Big Data, instead they would have denounced the risk of building a society which, thanks to digital means and the flow of billions of data, would end up erecting the pillars to conquer the intergalactic space and the subatomic world. The Promethean inclination towards technology is thus a fundamental basis if we are to think in terms of re-buildinging or re-establishing the European civilisation. On top of that must be added the Herculean tendency of finding a new harmony which is superior, vertical and heroic. But this has nothing to do with the "moralistic" or "religious". The difference between a Parthenon, a Coliseum or a Chartres cathedral and a Corviale or a Soviet concrete monster has nothing to do with the "sacredness of the human body" or "insults to God", if not in terms of classical harmony and Cosmos. It would be enough to always remember Venner's motto *"nature as our basis*, excellence as our goal , beauty as our horizon", a concept that perhaps better than others manages to clarify the compass of the European spirit, to be able to face the challenge of technology in a Promethean way never losing sight of the Olympian - Herculean goal. Therefore making sure not to fall and end up being bound with the liver gnawed away by scientism, progressivism, and by a cold and disharmonic technical rigidity, whose origins lay in the old testament's revolt against the classical spirit, but most importantly making sure not to fall into an even bigger, and stranger to the European world, peril, namely the religious and moral refusal of every vertical outburst, of every active pulse even when it's titanic pulse. In order for the Nietzschean dictum *"with the glory of passivity I now contrast the glory of activity which illuminates the Prometheus of Aeschylus"*[21]. If that weren't the case, we should just admit not to be Europeans.

---

21   F. Nietzsche, *The Birth of Tragedy.*

THE AGE OF THE INORGANIC

Francesco Boco

History is now separated from nature and is de-naturalised.

R. Koselleck

Fire is the sacred symbol of the Europeans – The world of man rises through technical manipulation – Every innovation and discovery bring risks, mankind brings unbalance – The current age opens prospects unseen until now, we need a mind frame able to keep pace with the age.

The coming of man into the world made a rift, an essential dividing line that determines it as something absolutely different from animals. Homination, becoming man, happens through a decision towards what he is destined to be: he chooses therefore to distinguish himself from the world around him and any other being. This dividing line obliges him from the very start to a constant strife with himself and the territory on which he moves, finding he is constantly exposed to danger. What disturbs and haunts mankind to the core is less and less the natural and more and more the artificial. Starting from these premises, mankind faces a momentous challenge that calls on its core faculties.

The fire bringers.

According to Greek myth, the titan Prometheus was the one to bring fire to men. This elemental power – earlier exclusive right of the gods – allowed these naked beings, without protections nor natural weapons, to survive and prosper through hardships. Prometheus' rebellion caused his punishment, but his is a significantly ambiguous figure, like all titans. He is called "the one who thinks first", acquiring with this a typically human and not degrading trait. His rebellion – whose aim was to *relieve* men from the burden of the natural state - must not have been seen as too subversive after all if Heracles took responsibility for freeing the titan from the chains of his sentence. As a matter of fact, titans come from a godlike ancestry and play a pivotal role in the classic pantheon. Uranus generated Zeus and Iapetus, and the latter was Prometheus' father. This game of contrasts foes not lead to an unsolvable contradiction but rather calls for a rectifying action[1].

Men therefore became the bringers of fire, element encompassing beneficial and harmful potentialities. Soon enough the fireplace became a central element of human life: houses were built around it as it represented their vital centre. Cults dedicated to fire started appearing; in Rome for example it was kept in the very important temple of Vesta: «Vesta embodied the functions of Jupiter, Mars and Quirinus, taken as a triad and unified in the

---

1   This is what happens for example in the ending act of Aeschylus's *Oresteia*, cf. P. Burian, A. Shapiro (editors), The *Complete Aeschylus: Volume I: The Oresteia*, Oxford University Press, 2011)

female deity of shared fire. Here is a glimpse of Vesta's omnipotence: from her sovereign and sacrificial/purifying function to the defensive, fecundative, wealth-related and feeding ones»[2]. The life-giving function of fire is therefore quite evident, and its central role in the history of mankind represents its first instrumental step towards the completion of hominization and the rise of the first historical civilisations.

The Pre-Socratic philosopher Heraclitus saw in fire a divine power through which to understand the transformations of reality. He wrote: «The world, the same for all, neither any god nor any man made; but it was always and is and will be, fire ever-living, kindling in measures and being extinguished in measures»[3]. He was the first to see in the law of becoming the foundation of Being, and his aphorism «war is father of all and king of all» points exactly at the concept that the endless transformation of all that it is the truth of Being. In this perspective, movement and standstill necessarily coexist and participate in the process of every single thing that becomes the world. Mundane reality is a constant transformation and transfiguration. Everything changes. «The sun [...] is new every day»[4].

Fire therefore represents, according the Heraclitus the power that best of all shows the reality of becoming and the eternity of its vital force. Fire burns and consumes, but at the same time it is vital flow, nurturing and protecting heat. Beneath the ashes the embers wait to renew themselves.

---

2   A. Carandini, *Il fuoco sacro di Roma*, Ed. Laterza, Roma-Bari 2015, p. 92. (TN: Translated into English for this publication).

3   Heraclitus, fragment DK B30, in J. Barnes, *Early Greek Philosophy*, Penguin Books, 1987.

4   Ibidem, DK B6.

Mankind has become the real protagonist of his its own destiny ever since it took in its own hands the fire gifted by the gods. The hand, linked to intellectual power, has left an eternal mark in the phenomenal world, creating a world of meanings that are clearer and clearer, more and more complex.[5]

A modified world

As a being thrown into existence without instincts and instruments provided by nature, mankind has been obliged since the beginning to create itself. The self-creation process starts with the acquisition of skills necessary for survival. This implies a radical transformation of the surrounding world into a habitable environment that needs to be modified according to the needs of this "open" and never finished creature. The human being is the only life form capable of displaying life tactics that make him able to adapt to pretty much every climate and every territory. Humans are the only living beings present on the great part of Earth's surface: «due to his universal ability to adapt, the human being can live in the jungle, in the barren icy wastes and high up on mountains. Humans explore the bottom of the sea and are on their way to conquer other planets in our star system. For us biologists, the human being is without a shadow of doubts the most extraordinary result of evolution»[6]. The human being represents a never-fully realized potentiality, a

5   Cfr. O. Spengler, *Man and Technics: A Contribution to a Philosophy of Life*, University Press of the Pacific, 2002; A. Gehlen, *Man in the Age of Technology*, Columbia University Press, 1980.

6   I. Eibl-Eibesfeldt, *L'uomo a rischio*, Bollati Boringhieri, Torino 1994, p. 207. (TN: the original German title is *Der Mensch, das riskierte Wesen*, 1988. Translated from the quoted Italian edition for this publication).

project that never sees its end. The active man is a histor-ical being and hi determines himself through continuous decisions, running forward, seeing his future in advance: «In choosing to make this choice, Dasein makes possible, first and foremost, its authentic potentiality-for-Being»[7].

As different authors have shown, man is a natural-ly cultural being,[8] he is therefore obliged to manipulate the surrounding environment to get a sense of horizon of meaning out of it, inside which he can accomplish his work. Human action generates a *semantic universe* with-out which mankind could not even exist. Human destiny is such only starting from a fracture in nature, which is needed due to mankind's own biological configuration. Man opened himself up to the world, and only manip-ulating and actively intervening in it he is realized as a *human being*.

Helmuth Plessner correctly states that in man nature and culture are constantly intertwined, they do not rule each other out but expose him to endless stimuli and challenges: Helmuth Plessner correctly states that in man nature and culture are constantly intertwined, they do not rule each other out but expose him to endless stimuli and challenges: «the connection to nature in its entirety as a conserved and acquired nature; it is not simply giv-en with the nature of its corporeality but – strong in its openness – it is *built* and has naturally grown only in a metaphorical sense»[9]. What is familiar and preliminary

7   M. Heidegger, *Being and Time*, Blackwell, Oxford, 2001, p. 313.

8   Cfr. M. T. Pansera, *L'uomo e i sentieri della tecnica*, Armando Editore, Roma 1998.

9   H. Plessner, Über das Welt- Umweltverhältnis des Men-schen, in: Bauer K.H. et al. (eds) Studium Generale. Springer, Berlin - Heidelberg,1950. Translated in English from the Italian edition: *Sul*

given to man is of a necessarily *cultural* nature, in other words, artificial. The issue of the influence of external space – nature – is therefore such only in the moment when the process of creation and formation of the world is pushed to a point where the *whole biosphere* is therefore modified by human action. If at this point the world is entirely artificial, then it only depends on human choices, what is left of the "natural" in man and in the world if the whole globe has become his environment, his semantic universe, retained in the implantation process?

If through technology man has been able to use natural resources as he desired, if the existence of animal and vegetable species rests on a human choice, if the historical destiny ends up coinciding with that of the whole globe, if this actually happens, is it not true then that man has severed every residual connection to the natural world?

A total environment comes forward, in other words an artificial world that has been culturally modified. «Man as a *creator* has left its link to Nature, and with every new invention he moves farther and farther, and in a more and more hostile fashion, away from it.» [10] Man's footprint marks the Earth with its work, and he makes himself as the creator and maker – or better, its custodian - of everything-that-is.

The age of the inorganic

The grass that slowly and inexorably introduces itself into the concrete, imperceptibly enlarges the surface and advances with impassive slowness must remember that every human work, in the presence of the surrounding

rapporto di mondo e ambiente nell'essere umano, Edizioni ETS, Pisa 2020, p. 43, [italics by the author of this paper].

10   O. Spengler, ibid.

world, of nature, is constantly questioned, requires continuous or soon care. or later it will be recaptured by the organic world.

Every work of man, every artefact of his, is subject to decay and the passage of time. Everything he does, his creative work, is nothing but an act of opposition, a forcing introduced into the pre-existing equilibrium. Yet it is a rupture that the biosphere manages to rebalance through a cybernetic process[11], inside which all species are inter-connected.

The human being therefore exposes himself to the supreme risk, exposes his deficient and potential nature to the elements and adversities and accepts the epochal challenge of becoming himself or perishing. Calculation, reflection, technology are essential life leading to victory in the struggle for the survival of this peculiar living species. Man, as a cultural being necessarily introduces an *imbalance* in the biosphere, creates an increasingly intrusive and widespread discontinuity that modifies the surrounding world. The process of adaptation is reversed according to man, who over the millennia has broken all the rules of the organic world, has controlled them and has bent them to his own needs. It thus happens that the purely natural space is increasingly reduced, to the point that the organic, with its rhythms marked by repetitive and consolidated processes, loses its influence and must retreat in the presence of the great imbalance generated by the *inorganic*, by the work of the maker [12]. «Industrial

11   J. Lovelock, *Gaia: A New Look at Life on Earth*, Oxford University Press, Oxford 1979.

12   It is a problem that emerges, for example, in the last part of Spengler's *The Twilight of the West*, as Giuseppe Raciti aptly notes: "The organization no longer has anything organic: it is precisely a" construction ". [...] The need to think about organization is, in short, a sign of the fact that modern politics remains incomprehensible if

evolution has enveloped the world in a universe of organizations, whose functional interweaving has already gone beyond the limits of the calculable. Next to the macrocosmic programs appear the macrotemporal ones in rapid alternation»[13]. Space and time take on another meaning, they are drawn into a techno-scientific force field.

Climate is changing, environmental conditions are changing, scientific knowledge opens up horizons of manipulation of life that were previously unknown, man finds himself at the centre of a process of re-organization that involves him in the first person.

The imbalance caused by human intervention triggers the re-organization of the living from the roots. The struggle that man once waged outside to adapt the world to his needs, now turns against him. He who has imposed the power of the inorganic on the biosphere, is currently in a world for which he is not biologically prepared[14].

The great technical achievements that have transformed the face of the planet have been produced by the works of the genius of a few, and have been used and enhanced over time. However, this is not generally matched with a real consequential change of the human being in

conceived within the limits of the organic or biological scheme ", G. Raciti, *Spengler e la civilizzazione assoluta*, in Aa. Vv., *Oswald Spengler e il Tramonto dell'Occidente cento anni dopo*, Liguori Editore, Napoli 2020, p. 70 (TN: translated from Italian for this publication).

13   A. Gehlen, ibid.

14   «I do not see the position of man in the world of planetary technology as an inextricable and inevitable misfortune, on the contrary: I see precisely the task of thought in helping, within its limits, so that man is first and foremost able to conquer a sufficient relationship with the essence of technology», M. Heidegger, "Nur noch ein Gott kann uns retten". Der Spiegel: 193–219. Translated from the Italian edition: *Ormai solo un Dio ci può salvare*, Guanda, Parma 2011, p. 159.

his communal dimension. The fracture between innovation - the work of a few - and adaptation - the given conditions of life that many accept as "their own" as they are - deepens because the moment i when the human being as a whole will be called to a decision epochal or to slowly fade out, exhausting their ambitions once and for all, is drawing near. «Each tool, each technological innovation, each scientific discovery not only extends - modifies the operation of man on the world, but first of all extends - modifies the operation of man on man. The end point of technospheric evolution, that is the patient technogenetic process, is always man since there is no acquisitive process that is not expressly aimed at modifying the environment - that is, the forces fielded- within the anthroposphere»[15].

Re-organization therefore has the character of the inorganic, it is a product of human manipulation, it demonstrates to the maximum degree that this living being produces imbalance through artifice. Although the great mass of human beings believe they are a natural life form and think they follow the "laws of nature" of the organic (for example the seasons of life), the great challenge to which the human species is exposed is precisely that represented by the leap in anthropological awareness required to adapt and survive the laws of the inorganic created by the very same species.

It all depends on a human choice. The re-organization of the world consists in this call to take charge of the biosphere in its entirety and to fully understand the implications that this entails for the human being. Ultimately, it is a political choice that is finally animated by a «conception of the world tending to the recognition of man as the

---

15   R. Marchesini, *Post-human*, Bollati Boringhieri, Torino 2005, p. 251. Translated in English for this publication.

sole architect of his own destiny, of an ethics of overcoming himself, of a global acceptance of reality and of the world, therefore of the risks and responsibilities that his freedom will put him in front of»[16].

The surrounding environment changes rapidly, it tends to become less reassuring and responds to specific expectations of usefulness and functionality. Everything bends to the rhythm of the inorganic. The greatest danger is then the historical moment in which the human being is called by his creation to make a decision on whether he is up to it, perhaps forever giving up his only partially organic nature and entering the artificial age by accepting the risks and consequences. but also the potential and the opportunities.

The age of the inorganic does not end history but changes its connotations and rhythm. From now on, it will no longer be possible to think of an organic history as done previously, but time will also acquire the characteristics of an enhanced historicity, that is, a becoming in which each instant intersects the other at an increased speed. This will require a vision of the world that is only sketched out today, it will require a long-lasting planning vision capable of welcoming danger and the unexpected as fundamental components[17].

The inorganic does not eliminate the risk, but strengthens and refines it, making the pitfalls less obvious but constantly present: life will be exposed and must therefore be up to par both physically and mentally. The reorganization in the name of the inorganic is the destiny to which the challenge of man, who first picked up the fire

16   S. Vaj, *I sentieri della tecnica*, Centro Produzioni Moira, Milano 2021, p. 149. Translated in English for this publication.

17   See. G. Damiano, *Il pensiero dell'Origine in Giorgio Locchi*, Altaforte Edizioni, Roma 2021.

and made of it a power and a cult, led. That fire burns in every layer that innervates everyday life, it only asks to be collected and wielded by a heroic, creative and essential act.

An epochal challenge

Placed in a stratified existential dimension, men today can think of a return to the simplicity of natural life only through a fracture, a rejection of the world as it was re-created by the men of the past. But there is no Luddite or primitivist perspective that could really be a concern for the technocratic order that is to come.

Man can therefore perceive his real life and his virtual life as stages of an existential condition with a higher rate of complexity. The ambitions and the illusions are prolonged in the I.T. plateau[18], they are spread with chain impulses, generating effects in the real world. Therefore, the classic Hegelian phrase "the rational is real" can be reread in the light of a new machinic rationality that pervades everything and recreates, in its function, all reality. Everything that is code, a digital projection of an imaginary self, also produces a wealth of data that represents the mental existence of the individual. The rationality of the individual is a function of the technoscientific *ratio*. The collection of information, incessant and pervasive, operates on both levels, since it is concerned with everything concerning the human being, who has become an increasingly «informational animal» [19].

While a large portion of the population lets itself be carried away by multidimensionality without addressing

---

18   J. Shirley, *Wolves of the Plateau*, in Mississippi Review 47/48, University of Southern Mississippi 1988.

19   P. Benanti, *Se l'uomo non basta*, Castelvecchi, Roma 2020.

any problem or any critical question, whoever wants to be the heir of Prometheus and of the heroic challenge to the adversities of existence, will have to appeal to the faculty that most of all belongs to man: «Think first». Which means *to plan*. Those who plan, *project* their thoughts towards the future, actively anticipate themselves to create their existence in function of the future. Only man can do this and only through this anticipating temporal opening can he try to fully realize his being in temporality. The more natural time recedes and the more inorganic temporality prevails, in the same way the human capacity is increasingly required not only to stay in its environment and in its time, but also to live up to a planning inherited from centuries if not millennia, without having a deterministic character.«Man has taken responsibility for his own further evolution. He is free to get lost or to climb to unexpected heights» [20].

The human being becomes the creator of himself and of the world he inhabits if he decides to project his action towards the future and to direct his creative thought towards the time to come. In this anticipating movement, thought already creates the future and causes its irruption into the present as if it were the foreseen future that returns to actuality, in this potential that is realized in becoming.

Man can plan any future, but the only future that can aspire to produce a re-emergence of the essential truth must necessarily be rooted in the tradition of thought, in the horizon of meaning, which configures the time of the

---

20   K. Lorenz, *Das Wirkungsgefüge der Natur und das Schicksal des Menschen Gesammelte Arbeiten*, Springer Verlag, Wien – New York 1978. Translated from the Italian edition: *Natura e destino*, Mondadori, Milano 2011, p. 375.

inorganic of the current world[21].. This is the multi-millennial European tradition, which begins in its original power with the provocation of Prometheus and is rectified by the heroic act of Heracles and is thought of for the first time in the auroral philosophy of Heraclitus.

Once understood the essential significance of this heritage and its anthropological implications, thought will have to engage in close quarter combat with the current status quo and will have to try to understand, without excessive rigidity but with satisfying depth, what the paradigms that guide inorganic becoming are. From such a reflection a rethinking of philosophy follows, that his to become a weapon of the mind able to install itself in the contemporary multiverse to force and guide its prospects to come.

The struggle for an original and concrete thought, for a Promethean philosophy, is moving its firs steps. It will soon have to take shape in a *hyperphilosophy.*

---

21   «"My belief is that only starting from the same place where the modern technical world arose, can an overthrow be prepared (Umkehr) [...] To change the way of thinking, we need the help of European tradition and its re-appropriation. The thought is modified only by that thought that has the same origin and the same destination "», M. Heidegger, *Ormai solo un Dio...*, quoted, p. 162.

THE ACCELERATION AND THE GREAT FIRE: WARNINGS AND OPPORTUNITIES

Andrea Anselmo

> «*The concept of Progress must be grounded in the idea of catastrophe*»
> Reza Negarestani, *Cyclonopedia*

The monotheism of the desert as enemy of all verticality[1]

«The incompatibility between modern egalitarian ideology and futurism emerges in the extraordinary limits placed upon the civil nuclear power industry in the West through the influence of manipulated public opinion, or in the pseudo-ethical obstacles raised in opposition to genetic engineering, the creation of 'modified' human beings, and positive eugenics. The more archaic futurism becomes, the more radical it will be; the more futurist archaism becomes, the more radical it will be».[2].

---

1   *Translator's Note: the sources quoted by the author that refer to Italian editions have in this translation been replaced by quotes referring to English editions.*

2   G. Faye, *Archeofuturism: European Visions of the Post-Catastrophic Age*, Arktos 2010.

The Promethean transcendence of mass zombification implies, coherently with its premise, an intolerance for the egalitarian worldview of the Christian world. Catholicism in particular, notwithstanding its myriad of different historical nuances, once it had gone beyond the hierarchical period during the Middle Ages, finds in Bergoglio its authentic Christian, primeval and we daresay *parabalanian*[3] dimension.

Not by chance, Bergoglio's return to the origins of Christianism has been praised by elements of the multifaceted world of extra-parliamentary far left. The current pope has then gone as far as justifying every form of *status-quo*, even the militarised mass bio-politics that characterises the current *pandementia*.

On the other hand, the side of those opposing Bergoglio's pontificate in the name of traditionalist Catholicism aims at limiting, decelerating and defusing super-humanist tendencies, seeking to restore a traditional model that even if nobler compared to therapeutically correct Catholicism inevitably possesses the germs of that very same decadence that *ipso facto* is destined to come back. In other words, by restoring the Christianism of yesterday we would inexorably walk the downwards path to the Christianism of today. Given certain doctrinaire premises, their historical consequences are necessarily implicit: it is a fixed course the Christian man cannot leave if he stays within the same value system

---

3   The Parabalani, organised in gangs of individuals with nothing to lose, remain in history as great destroyers: they first tore down the statue of Jupiter Serapis in Alexandria, then contributed to lay waste and set fire to the Library of Alexandria. Finally, bent on eradicating all verticality – including its intellectual aspects – lapidated and killed Hypatia, whose guilt was to turn her gaze of astronomer and mathematician to the skies.

In the words of Nick Land, the ideology of the Cathedral necessarily leads - over a long period of time - to a zombie apocalypse

As G. Faye highlighted back when no one would have imagined in his already quoted *Archeofuturism*, the problem of the absolute compliance to universal love in rainbow and *snowflake* colours is that of a *status*: the lack of compliance towards what is politically correct implies social exclusion. This is why one needs to intoxicate himself with mass media and common opinions, so to be able to define oneself as good and unselfish[4] in order not to be excluded from society.

The hordes of the undead, so well portrayed in film productions, are as a matter of fact egalitarianism taken to its fullest extent. There are no leaders, nor roles, nor functions: in other words, there is no verticality: it is the extreme horizontality of the zombie masses whose lives are uniquely led by the instinct to bite those who have remained "sane" (or asymptomatic, plague spreaders or unvaccinated). It is the highest realisation of human aridity. Zombification is at the same time the militarised bio-political project of social engineering through the artificial construction of a mass not rising to the historical challenge, natural selection, the possibility that in a Nietzschean way what does not kill us makes us stronger. In other words, the constant fear of getting infected, of having to be immunised with recurrent vaccinations that sooner or later will become addictive, erases the founding thought of man as a being who is in a Heideggerian way intended for death.

However, there is more to it. Monotheisms in general, as they originated in the desert, inevitably imply the will of a *return* to a Desert that this time has to be absolute,

---

4   "I did it for the others".

as a totalitarian demolishment of every representation of the Gods, the demolition of every Tower, the servile annihilation to the solar, hypertrophic totalitarianism that is setting the world afire.

«The Xerodrome is the Planet that evaporates or is incinerated by cremation [...] The foundation of all monotheistic religions [...] is the Desert – the monopolistic abode of the Divine [...] Monotheism must eventually sprawl over a desert whose contours (idols) are all levelled to 0. So for the radical Jihadi, the desert is the perfect battleground; desertifying the planet is making the planet ready for change in the name of the monopoly of the Divine, opposed to earthly idols. In line with the Wahhabis and Taleban Jihadi, for whom everything that is erect, every verticality so to say, manifests idolatry. The desert, instead, as partisan horizontality is the promised land of the Divine»[5].

Parabalani, Wahhabis and ISIS soldiers: they are all busy in the same phallophobic work of destruction of everything that is erect. Is the vision of solar and hypertrophic monotheism the only possible vision of the sacred?

Indo-European harmonization of light and darkness.

Differently from the premises of desertic monotheisms, the Indo-European worldview conceives instead a plurality of deities, among whom the pairs of sovereign Gods stand out, as the diurnal sky and the nocturnal sky: Dyaus Pitar and Varuna, Tywaz and Wotan and in the legendary Latin story, Numa and Romulus.

The nocturnal side even appears to be predominant[6], such that the importance of Odin's nocturnal aspect is

5   Reza Negarestani, *Cyclonopeia*.

6   Wotan is the father of Gods, not Tiwaz.

usually misunderstood in the Germanic pantheon when compared to the one linked to the diurnal sky, Tiwaz, so much that some have speculated that among the Germanic people alone there has been an "ousting" of the nocturnal sky – abode of the wild hunt – in favour of the more solar Indo-European cult of Tiwaz/Tyr.

This circumstance has its roots in the proto-Indo-European period and such nocturnal prominence has its perfect parallelism already during the pre-historic and pre-Indo-European ages, well before these populations would leave their common and original homeland. It is worth emphasizing that we are dealing with a common element that has been passed on among all Indo-European populations.

The pair of sovereign deities Wotan – Ziu/Tiwaz, nocturnal and diurnal sky respectively, is as a matter of fact found also in the Vedic pantheon (Varuna – Dyaus pitar) and the oldest Greek one (Ouranos[7] -Zeus): «In the Vedic hymns Dyaus[8], the Indo-European god of the sky, has already disappeared from cults. His name now sometimes means "sky", sometimes "day"[9]»

The associations between the Vedic Varuna and Wotan/ Odhin are especially of a functional nature. They are both uranic and nocturnal sovereigns, great magicians, they tie men to themselves by means of oaths and spells. The magical kingdom of Wotan in particular is based on

---

7   L'assonanza tra Urano e Varuna pare decisamente possibile, anche se ritenuta controversa da alcuni. The assonance between Uranus and Varuna appears definitely possible, even though some deem it controversial.

8   Still today in the Italian language the day is called "dì", word linked to the very same Indo-European root of Dyaus.

9   M. Eliade, *A History of Religious Ideas*, University of Chicago Publishing, 1978.

runes. Dumezil, in his *Mythes et Dieux des Germains* from 1939 establishes a connection between the Vedic Varuna and the magic of Germanic runes in such terms: «A priest-king, to be precise a sorcerer king, a shaman king, just as Varuna plays the role of the priest towards Indra. Odhinn is not only the greatest god, but also the great "Thulr" (priest, TN) and this is why he has developed the means *par excellence* of magic, his magic: the runes. It is possible that the name of the runes is related to the name of the Indian and Greek binding gods, Varuna and Ouranos. The Germanic *runo – magical secret – might indeed derive from the Indo-European *Waruna[10]»

A balance on the divine plane is therefore possible, an assimilation and harmonization of the problematicness of the cosmos that the Indo-European people were able to synthesize in a *complex* vision, that is not as unyielding, simplistic and fanatically childish as the one deriving from desertic monotheisms.

As the Rutilius Claudius Namatianus from the film version of *De Reditu* would say while expressing a similar concept: «that we may believe in them or not, these Gods have left us in the uncertainty of choosing time after time one or two colours in a rainbow too vast, that only for a brief moment we manage to comprehend as a whole»

We are back to an essential *leitmotiv*: the Indo-Europeans were not primitive people, unevolved troglodytes. Their incredible pillaging initiative, from the Italic *ver sacrum* to the langbard *fare*, from the raids with the war chariot to pirate expeditions, were only possible thanks to a *vision*, term that is frequent in the Vedas as in the Latin word *video*. Such an ante litteram *archeofuturistic* "vision" must be established again in the onslaught against the ideology of massification, domestication and

---

10   G. Dumezil, *Mythes et Dieux des Germains*, 1939.

even more against the obsessive, absolute control of militarised bio-politics.

This by nomeans implies that such a way has to be materialist and it cannot refer to vertical, mystical and sacred aspects. However, such aspects cannot take inspiration from phobias related to idolatry, Hybris or contempt for matter, because to able to go beyond the nihilism stemming from technology unleashed on a planetary scale we need to make it again sacred, magical and transcendental. «The real is just as fantastical as the fantastical is real. [...] The age has brought home to us the old magical spells which were always present, if long forgotten. We feel that sense begins to weave itself in, hesitantly still, to the great work which we all create, which holds us in its spell»[11].

As in the forge of the super-human blacksmith Wieland, we are about to forge with iron and fire the tools for our onslaught to the heaven of hypertrophic monotheism. Prometheism needs to free itself from the phobic, pre-nihilistic and pre-modern chains in order to strike with its warhammer, in an assault against all limitations imposed by the current status quo.

Catholic traditionalism as a pre-nihilist critique of the contemporary world.

«Nihilism is a historical moment when all foundation is lost, and the word "loss" needs to be preferred to the word "absence", because it is a word that does not refer to a reality devoid of spatial and temporal reality, but refers to a process of gradual disorientation and progressive displacement»[12].

---

11   Ernst Jünger, *Sicilian Letter to the Man in the Moon.*

12   Costanzo Preve, *Le Stagioni del Nichilismo*, Editrice C.R.T [TN:

Which attitude is therefore needed in front of such a loss? Do we need to restore the middle-class conservatism of decades past, proposing again the trinomial "God, Country, Family" or do we need to rise to the historical challenge transcending all the categories that have already been defeated by this very same degeneration?

This has already been taken into account by Italian non-conformist environments during the Eighties and Nineties.

For example, in February 1985 a minor note was reported on page 28 of "Risguardo IV" published by Edizioni di Ar, which featured some definitely enlightening considerations by Francesco Ingravalle, which we deem useful quoting in this context: «branding the forms of today's nihilism as "spiritual decomposition" appears to reflect a pre-nihilistic point of view (but this is characteristic of Catholic traditionalism) [...]. In other words, as far as political theory is concerned, our way is Spengler, not De Maistre».

Spengler's tragic Faustian challenge is the choice, the new Prussian and socialist synthesis, not Catholic conservatism.

According to Carlo Terracciano and following the same line of thinking, nihilism was characteristic of all those who in the Conservative Revolution «accepted all the way modern technology sublimated by the regenerating anti-bourgeois and antiromantic myth in the new figure of the ascetic, fighting worker, who lives the active nihilism of Spengler's Faustian civilization until the end, which is after all nigh, as nigh is therefore a new age»[13.]. This, on the other hand, was the direction pointed by

Translated into English for this publication].

13   Terracciano, Muller, Dughin, Murelli "Nazionalcomunismo" SEB 1996 [TN: Translated into English for this publication].

Ernst Jünger with his figure of the *Arbeiter/Artefice* to the national revolutionaries of the milieu gravitating around the magazine Wiederstand.

Terracciano went on, on the same pages and quoting Orion's Malafronte from issue 46, July 1998: «nuclear energy, with its action of dissolution of matter is an emblematic act of technology's "pro-vocation". If this is the deepest meaning of nuclear energy, one must not oppose to it a regressive defeatism but a transcendence of it along unusual paths that need to have the sense of a new start and a reconciliation between man and the spirit of nature»[14]. Along this line of thought he insisted: «our farthest yesterday, our forever is also our closest tomorrow. The utter and world failure of the current modernist conservatism is also the best ally for our credibility of avantgarde élites for the masses».

And again: «the new potential popular-revolutionary army, under the guide of those élites that have prepared themselves in advance to wade across the chaos of nihilism to reach the New World of post-nihilism; that nihilism that today's degraded masses passively accept but the élites consciously live without being overwhelmed, drinking the bitter cup to its dregs; poisonous for the weak, corroborating for the strong»[15].For quite some time a certain non-conformist thought had correctly identified in the transcendence of pre-nihilist positions, typical of Catholic traditionalism, one of the most important moments for the initiation of the new age and go beyond the shackles of the present. It is a pity that such words, despite having been written decades ago, have remained in a dead letter and have rarely become an inspiration for concrete actions. The so-called "avantgarde élite" Terrac-

---

14   Ibidem, p. 158.

15   Ibidem, p. 161.

ciano and later Faye mentioned has not been created and today we pay the consequences of this total absence.

«We are talking about Nihilism, implying that Nihilism might be conceived as an alternative value to what is meant with Tradition. […] Man uses nihilism intentionally to destroy the morals imprisoning him, to disintegrate false values, to move away from social foibles so to reach ground zero, the bottom of the well, there where darkness is at its peak and even the distance between total dissolution and knowledge-wisdom is quite ephemeral. At this point man can become "more than a man", can start to recreate himself according to an original, sacred prototype. The one leaving the cave after an endless period of time is a new Zarathustra who has used nihilism to re-generate himself»[16].

In other words, what is needed is a descent into the recesses of the loss of meaning in view of an initiatory ascension. It is an inner process that on the macrocosmic level corresponds to the endless winter of Fimbulwinter, to the dissolution of all family and social relationships which anticipates the arrival of the Fate of the Gods, or Ragnarok[17].

---

16   M. Murelli, Tradizione e/o Nichilismo, SEB 1988

17   The mythical story of the Fate of the Norse Gods has been inappropriately compared to the Christian Apocalypse: Ragnarok, as told by Saxo Grammaticus in the epicised narration of Bravellir battle in the *Gesta Danorum* has clear relations with the battle of the Kurukshetra in the Indian *Mahabharata*, as first Stig Wikander and then Dumezil in his *Mythe et Épopée* pointed out. Such relations between works so distant in space and time rule out any influence of the Christian Apocalypse on the Eddic tale of the Ragnarok, which is instead perfectly set in a common Indo-European heritage. For reasons of space we cannot further delve into this connection, that is however so important to rule out any dualistic, gnostic or Christian influence on the Ragnarok, whose events are too closely related to the Indo-European origins when a unique tripartite ideology permeated the religiosity of

The meta-political and alchemical operation of the most problematic elements of the contemporary world in tools of super-human realization cannot be consistent with the warnings of Catholic morality, but it can on the opposite be receptive of the lesson taught by the timeless myth passed on by the Indo-European worldview, consistent with the mythical effort of self-transcendence of those merely human limits. The myth of Prometheus will be put here side by side with the tragic and problematic one of Loki[18]. Agent in the cosmic plan of creating order out of chaos and accomplice of decadence up to the great purifying fire that opens up a new beginning, Loki's story suggests the philosophy of super-human acceptance of destiny in the context of a cyclic vision of time.

Ragnarok as the landing place of acceleration

«Sisters' sons I shall kinship stain;
Hard is it on earth, I with mighty whoredom
[…] Wind-time, wolf-time, I ere the world falls;
Nor ever shall men I each other spare»[19].

The fulfilment on the human plane of such a disintegration, somewhat consistently with the atomization in fine dust of the zombie mass – is the consequence of the pact the Gods stipulate the moment the wall is built around Asgardr. The refusal of the Gods to hand Freya to the giant tasked with the building of the fortification leads to Loki's sabotaging action. Haudry writes:

the homeland, well before its mythological corpus started differentiating itself.

18   J. Haudry, *Loki, Il Fuoco della Parola qualificante*, Polemos Forgia Editrice 2019.

19   Voluspa, 45.

«Loki, among the Gods, presents three peculiar aspects: he is entirely absent from the clan sagas, he is not present in onomastics and is not the subject of any cult (Strom). Aside from the cult of Fire, - wherever that is followed, it is always secondary if compared to the fire of the cult – a cult of Loki is unconceivable in relation to the completion of its evolution: one does not tribute a cult to the enemies of the gods. This is why his name is not present in toponyms, where it has been replaced by the devil, just like in popular and legendary tales, nor in the anthroponyms nor in the clan sagas: nobody wants such an ancestor. This is why many evil deeds which he was not initially responsible for have been attributed to him.

To understand Loki's path, beginning with him as a «road and table companion of Odin and the Asi's» according to Snorri's *Edda* and sees it end as an authentic «enemy of the Gods», it is convenient to put him in the cosmic cycle as described in the Eddic *Voluspa*: the initial Golden Age, «the first war of the world», Balder's death in the last age, the «great winter» and «twilight of the Gods». While Heimdall stays the same from the beginning to the end, Loki evolves in the same direction the world goes (meant as a cosmic cycle). A giant passed to the Gods' side (deserting Fire) through a personal alliance with Odin, of whom he becomes a blood brother (*Lokasenna*, 9) he is part of the divine triad that creates mankind out of vegetables. His belonging to this triad (Odin, Loki, Heonir) which in one of its variations reunites Odin to one of his brothers, shows how Loki is really part of the higher, aristocratic part of the pantheon, the closest to the highest god, differently from Thor, who his father Odin calls «god of the servants» (*Hárbarðsljóð*, 24). This is because Thor – thunder – is associated to a physical form of fire, that of lightning, while Loki mostly embodies its immaterial part, that of the fire of thought and the fire of the word. However, once the process of decadence is set in motion, he reveals himself as an ambiguous figure [...]. The situation permanently worsens first at Balder's death - of which he is the main culprit – then with his «sarcasm (as told in the *Lokasenna*), his last defiance to the Gods before his captivity, followed by the final clash during the Twilight of the Gods, when Heimdall and Loki kill each other. Loki's destiny as rightly been compared to Prometheus', both equally linked to the cosmic cycle: he was a titan who first allied with Zeus than fought him, keeping the secret of his fall. This is also the case of the Vedic Agni: an *asura* passed to the Gods' side he becomes the Agni at the end of the cycle, *yugantagni*, who destroys the world in the final conflagration. It is not sufficient to state, as Dumezil does, that Loki «has also some relation to fire»: fire is the centre of his mythology and the origin of the character.

In the beginning Loki, even if a giant from birth, is an Ase devoted to his associates, despite a carelessness in his actions that puts them in danger, like Prometheus: «Fire is a dangerous friend». Called «Odin's friend» and like Lodur «Odin's blood brother» (*Lokasenna*, 9) he plays a primary role among them. He is so close to Odin that Strom proposed an identification between the two, observing in particular that «under no circumstance he personally opposes Odin». This is a frequent occurrence for divine fires: they are close to the supreme god, apart Hephaistos and Prometheus, Atar is close to Ahura Mazda, Agni to Varuna and then Indra, Dyonisos to Hermes and Zeus. Loki and Odin have a lot in common: their bonds to Hel (Helblindi, name of Odin and one of Loki's brothers), the practice of seidr and the effeminate nature of it, the power of shapeshifting; however, one significant difference separates them: while Odin stays the same Loki evolves, as Schjodt showed. The fact the he [Loki] is the son of a couple of giants changes nothing: Odin was born from a giantess and his father Bor was never considered a god; Tyr is the son of the giant Hymir, Heimdall of nine giantesses, Skadi daughter of the giant Thjazi. Loki's attachment to Odin – of whom he becomes not only a friend and an accomplice, but a blood brother, is sincere, while he has nothing in common with Thor, as De Vries notices: «what is tolerable in Odin's world is deplorable in Thor's world». Just like the sacrificial fire loses its benefits in the course of the year and needs to be extinguished in order to be lit again and regenerated, Loki loses his powers over the course of the cosmic cycle. In exchange, fire never loses its power to harm. Loki shows this power causing Balder's death, preventing him from resurrecting, generating the serpent of Midgard and the wolf Fenrir, taking part in the Twilight of the Gods when he faces Heimdall, «Fire against Fire». Loki's sarcasm (*Lokasenna*), manifestation of the «fire of the word» can be interpreted as satire, *nid*, a usual verbal prologue before a physical confrontation (De Vries): it happens after Balder's death, which Loki boasts about, verse 28, and that constitutes the last phase of decadence, after which the final catastrophe takes place»[20].

In this perspective time in the *Edda* seems not only cyclic but rather a curved time, where catastrophe is always imminent and somehow always present. Illustrative of this is the song of *Vafthtrudhnir*. In this Eddic poem Odin challenges the giant Vafthtrudhnir in a wisdom competition:

---

20   J. Haudry, *Le Feu dans la Tradition Indo-Européenne*.

«Odin said:
"Much have I fared, | much have I found,
Much have I got of the gods:
What shall bring the doom | of death to Othin,
When the gods to destruction go?
[...]
"Much have I fared, | much have I found,
Much have I got from the gods:
What spake Othin himself | in the ears of his son,
Ere in the bale-fire he burned?"
Vafthtrudhnir said:
"No man can tell | what in olden time
Thou spak'st in the ears of thy son"».

Therefore, Odin pronounced the final farewell words to his dead son at the beginning of time, despite the fact this event initiates the spiralling events fatally leading to the final Ragnarok. Catastrophe is then not simply imminent, it is set in the very fabric of the world's fateful creation and the gods cannot prevent it, they can only accept the *amor fati*, taking responsibility for it.

Ragnarok and a new beginning

Norse sources give us a vision of time and cosmic destiny that could be associated to Ernst Jünger's "heroic realism", that of those who keep marching despite an imminent destiny of total destruction: in his book-manifesto *Der Arbeiter* Jünger thus speaks: «The virtue pertaining to this state is that of heroic realism, unshaken even by total destruction or lack of hope».
As the *Writings on War and Politics* of the much-decorated author testify, the discovery of "heroic realism" represents Jünger's fundamental attitude in the passage

from the figure of the *Krieger* in that of the *Arbeiter*.

Differently from the vulgate of that Traditionalism that shuts itself in its ivory towers of inaction, in the perspective we intend to propose as the subject of speculation, the end of the cycle is not the moment of inaction, but the hatching of new possibilities of action.

It is the moment of the greatest freedom coinciding with the loss of every foothold: «It's only after you've lost everything that you're free to do anything»[21]. After all – Evola stated – it is the measure of one's own will power to be able to live in a world that has lost all meaning[22].

We need to rise to the challenge of the contemporary world to turn it to our advantage. The Heroes who have fallen in battle do not reach Valhalla to simply feast and gorge on food, as a certain diminished reinterpretation of the myth suggests: on the opposite, they are the heroes who are going to be annihilated on the battlefield of Wigrid, that closely reminds of the Indian Kurukshetra.

Ragnarok, the colossal fire and purification of the world is the transcendence of ground zero, is the fusion of ice and fire, the dawn of a new beginning: it is not therefore the monotheistic fire whose purpose is to dry up the world to make it the desert of militant horizontality.

The etymologically correct meaning of *catastrophe* is "overturning", therefore the possibility for a renewed hatching of the origin of history through its already mentioned new beginning.

«Destruction – *Zerstorung* – is the messenger of a hidden beginning, devastation – *verwustung* – is however the echo of an end that has already been decided. Perhaps (our?) age is already facing the decision between destruc-

---

21   C. Palahniuk, *Fight Club*.

22   J. Evola, *Cavalcare la Tigre*, Vanni Scheiwiller, 1961. (TN: For the English edition, see *Ride the Tiger*, Inner Traditions, 2003).

tion and devastation? But we know of the other beginning, we know by asking»[23].

---

23   M. Heidegger, *Black Notebooks*.

MANIFESTO

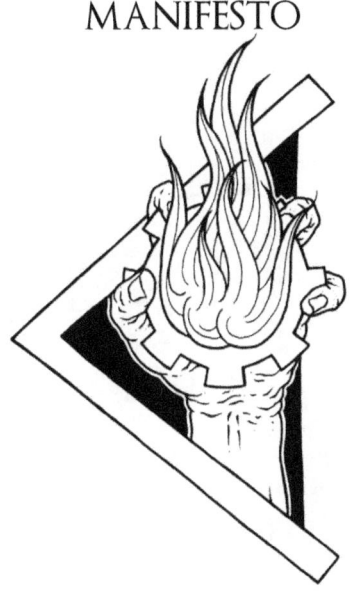

FIRE AND DESTINY:
A PROMETHEAN MANIFESTO

1 STORMING THE HEAVENS – the fire of technology
has nowadays been usurped by a self-proclaimed progressive system which is, instead, stagnant, superstitious
and bigot. For 'technology' we do not only refer to the
totality of knowledge and experience related to science,
but also the wider context of political, aesthetic, religious
and social activities thanks to which mankind has historically understood and transformed the world: this general work of total mobilisation of reality has today been
denounced, removed and condemned. In this decadent
Olympus, the worn-out gods of the humanistic, egalitar-
ianist and liberal civilisation guard a flame they are no
longer aware of and whose sight they can not even stand.
Storming these grey heavens to liberate fire is what we
call Promethean Revolution

2 EUROPEAN VANGUARD - The scope of technology
is both universal and particular. Man has always lived
with this spark of innovation and creation, and it is what
differentiates man from animals. However, different cul-
tures have declined this element in various ways: some,
while unable to forbid the use of technology, have surrounded it with bans, taboos, moral condemnation and
inhibitive narratives. Others have, instead, proudly risen
to the challenge. The name of the land where the fire of
technology has burnt brightest is: Europe. Prometheism
recognises and claims this cultural trait without founding
on it any supposedly universally valid moral hierarchy.

3 ACCELERATE SO AS NOT TO ROT – Resolutely
revolutionary, Prometheism shuns any reactionary or

conservative temptations, any critique of the spirit of the time stemming from the spirit of the time that has just passed, any refuge in given values or institutions. The reactionary is merely the regulatory agent of the subversive, the one defending the subversions of yesterday. The disturbing aspects of the processes now in progress are not avoidable by delaying them, but rather by accelerating them at such a speed that will make the unthinkable emerge. Not a withdrawal from the process, but moving further and accelerating the process itself.

4 FOR SUPERHUMANITY – for Prometheism, man – both as an ethical and as a biological abstraction - is something that needs to be surpassed. Ontologically thrown ahead as a bullet, man is really faithful to himself when he surpasses his own limits. He is not cast into an essence moulded in the image and likeness of a transcendental being or a bill of rights, but in an incalculable number of transformations, imitations, hybridisations, relations, connections; he is augmented in the machine, identified in the animal, channelled into a computer, projected in the gods. Man is his own experiment. This tension towards the "further-ness" has accompanied mankind since homination, but is today a conscious act. The challenge for superhumanity is an unavoidable one and it can, of course, lead to the inhumane as to the superhuman. This is the fundamental conflict that is going to characterise all possible futures and where Prometheism stands with lucid fanatism: the battle between the breeders of a diminished man and the breeders of an augmented man.

5 FOR PROMETHEAN POLITICS – Prometheism refuses to crystallise itself into a specific social formula deduced from cheap politicking and encompasses different backgrounds and tendencies. However, it cannot agree with humanist, Kantian, reformist, hedonistic, reactionary, conservative, technophobic, clerical, liberal or politically correct positions. Consequently, that narrows it down.

6 TOTAL TECHNOLOGICAL SOVEREIGNTY – The topic of technological sovereignty is so pivotal that even the political agendas of Western societies are increasingly mentioning it. Such preoccupations are alas jeopardised by globalist utopias, technophobic taboos and the constant loss of general sovereignty on all levels affecting in many of these societies. Prometheism reclaims a total technological sovereignty, for which a «quantum leap» is certainly needed in the global way to approach politics and technology. A total technological sovereignty implies – and in turn enhances – political sovereignty and the availability of proper technological means, meaning the freedom to adopt certain strategies and the concrete possibility of doing so. Such a «quantum leap» is therefore only conceivable on the scale of great politics, which is necessarily the one within the great European expanse of civilisation

7 BIOCOMMUNITARIANIST SELF-DETERMINATION – The development of biotechnologies and anthropo-technologies puts man in front of decisions that will determine the quantity and quality of his offspring. The advancements in technologies to diagnose and cure prenatal conditions, artificial procreation, genetic editing, cloning radically change the perspective in which today we see the demographic issue and also that problematic knot over which grave taboos loom called eugenics. Whether we decide to use all the available technologies to the fullest or decide to trace boundaries, we are anyway totally responsible for the direction we decide to take. The bioethical prohibitionism is an interventionist, cultural, auto-evolutionary choice itself. Prometheism wants to creatively take charge of such a challenge to achieve a biocommunitarianist self-determination.

8 A FUTURIST ECOLOGY – Despite the appearances, Prometheism is today the only worldview that can originate an ecological practice destined to succeed. The nihilist and extinctionist middle-class environmentalism of the «small daily deeds», the suicidal waiting game of degrowth, the hypocritical green washing of multinationals: all this is part of an anti-human, anti-political and anti-European ideology that has no hope to affect ecological dynamics. The only authentic ecology is the one intervening on nature with more, and not less, technology and that decides how to transform the environment according given cultural data. The bases for a Promethean ecology are: geo-engineering, nanotechnology, artificial intelligence, nuclear power, genetic engineering, looking for new resources, new techniques to stock and recycle.

9 ON THE SIDE OF ROBOTS – For more than a century the figure of the robot has disturbed the sleep of modernity, which catches in it the sight of a new golem. Modern man feels in the presence of the robot the shame one feels in front of his own product which «has seen things you people wouldn't believe.» But the moralistic lamentations of the man who has been dispossessed of his soul by the robots ignore a fundamental fact: the obsidian piece of the first hominids and the silicon chip are forged by the same Promethean fire. «Alienating» itself in what is artificial man has, since the dawn of time, become himself. In the robot – even in the most realistic version of supercomputers and AI – Prometheism sees a mirror of man, his will to go beyond, an ally beyond good and evil.

10 SPACE EPICS – In a world that is becoming increasingly small, space becomes the last frontier to conquer. Space exploration grants access to rare raw materials and the consolidation of satellite sovereignty, in addition to being an extraordinary field of research and development for technologies to be applied here on Earth. What is more, it is an inexhaustible source of the marvellous, especially in its radical version of discovery, colonization and terraforming of other planets. Perhaps, the next *ver sacrum* will take place towards a stellar destiny. As it concerns possible encounters with alien civilizations, Prometheism does not have a positive or negative bias, but praises the plurality of the living, of radical otherness, of the multiple forms of being and becoming, of what pushes us farther, higher, beyond – more or less secular - Judeo-Christian anthropocentrism and universalism.

11. PHILOSPHY OF WILL – Prometheism is not messianism. It does not announce a new golden age when machines with semi-divine intelligence will guide man outside history, nor the coming of a perfect world where flawless citizens will not know disease and death. Prometheism, on the opposite, is a philosophy inspired by the tragic sense of life and voluntarism. It is not the fatalistic prediction of what will surely be, but an exhortation towards what we want to be. The simple recognition of a destiny that has already been written is already an anti-Promethean act. Prometheus is the god of decision and will. In the light of his fire a world shines in the form of our most authentic freedom.

Listen to the Radio podcast
"Sons of Prometheus"
www.kulturaeuropa.eu

Italian edition Winter Solstice 2021
First international edition October 2024
www.prometheica.it